Because, Honestly

a series to tell you how I
feel when I don't know
how else to say it

BY
MELODY HANSEN

FOR YOU

IT STARTED WITH ONE

THIS ONE

THE SUN IS IN MY EYE

THIS IS THE

ONLY WAY

I KNOW

HOW TO MAKE MY HEART

FEEL

LIGHTER

YOU LIKED MY DRAWING AND
SO DID I

HI   CAN   WE   TALK ?

I REALIZED

THERE IS NO SHAME IN BEING HONEST

THERE IS NO SHAME IN BEING VULNERABLE

IT'S THE BEAUTY

      OF BEING HUMAN

YOU'RE ON MY MIND

I'M SCARED OF GROWING UP

WITHOUT YOU

MY OTHER HALF

WENT FOR A WALK

sometimes

I WISH
I WASN'T
A LONE.

LESS STUFF

MORE HEART

WE TALK BUT I CAN'T SEE YOU

IT'S OVERWHELMING

I LOST MY WAY ,
BUT YOU DIDN'T
LOSE ME

(I WON'T LOSE YOU)

YOU

(QUIET HEART)

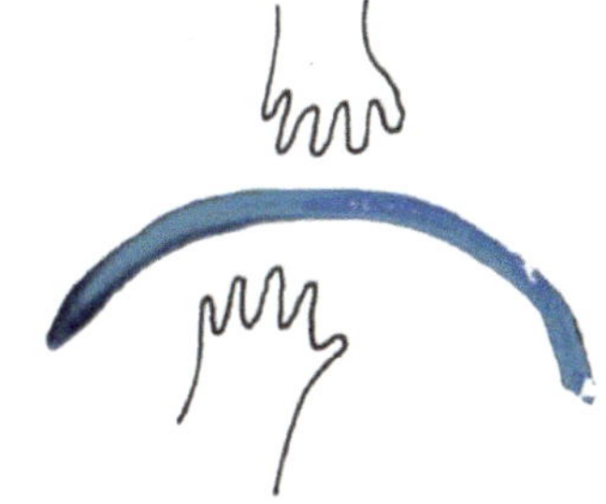

I CAN'T REACH YOU

(CLOSE YOUR EYES)

I CAN'T FIND HOME

(BREATHE)

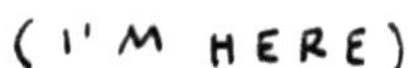
(I'M HERE)

YOU HAVE A NICE
HEART

I'M STILL GROWING

I LIKE IT
SO I WEAR IT

HOW ABOUT NO

I SEE GOLD IN YOU

THE SCARS ON YOUR SKIN,
    THE BROKEN PIECES OF
YOUR HEART

ARE LOVED

feel break heal feel
break heal feel break
heal feel break heal
feel break heal feel
break heal feel break
heal feel break heal
feel break heal feel
break heal

"HUMAN"

I RAN OUT
OF IDEAS

I DON'T KNOW

TO BE HUMAN IN PUBLIC,
WHAT A TABOO

EVERYBODY'S WATCHING
EVERYBODY

I ASKED THE GIRL
ON INSTAGRAM
HOW HER DAY WAS GOING
BUT NOT THE GIRL
SITTING BESIDE ME

I WANT TO BE MORE THAN AN ONLINE
PRESENCE

I WANT TO SAY SOMETHING

(SAY SOMETHING)

I WANT CHANGE,
BUT I DON'T WANT TO CHANGE
MY MIND

I ALWAYS LET
OTHER PEOPLE LEAD
BECAUSE I WAS TOO SCARED.

UNTIL

I DID SOMETHING BY MYSELF
AND REALIZED I HAD
GOOD IDEAS.

(SAY SOMETHING)

I KNOW

I KNOW

I NO

I NO

No

N

I   CARE.

TIME WILL TELL
BUT I CAN'T HEAR HER

WAITING ON THAT TEXT
I WASN'T EXPECTING

BEING SERIOUS IS TOO VULNERABLE

SO I LAUGH

HONESTY

is

POWERFUL

I'D RATHER

MAKE AN IMPACT

ON YOUR

HEART

THAN YOUR

EYES.

IT'S NOT ABOUT ME

I WEAR A HAT
TO KEEP MY ▬▬ WARM
IDEAS

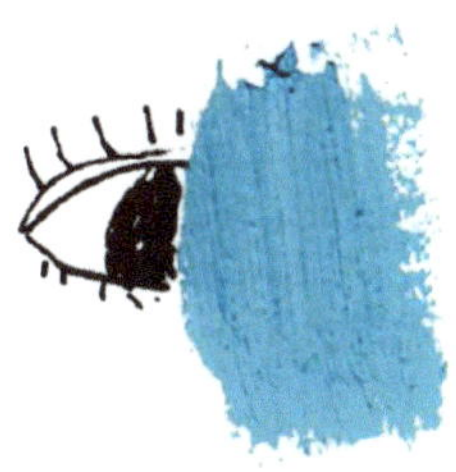

TEARS DON'T MEAN

I'M WEAK

DON'T APOLOGIZE

FOR FEELING

SOMETHING OR A LOT

strangers   lovers   strangers
lovers   strangers   strangers
strangers   ~~lovers~~   strangers
lovers   lovers   strangers
~~strangers~~   ~~lovers~~   strangers

NOT NOW

I CARRY YOU INSIDE
OF MY HEARTD

I DO MY BEST
SO YOU DON'T REPLACE ME

YOU FOUND SOMEONE ELSE

MY MIND LOOKS LIKE YOU
NOW I FORGOT WHAT
I LOOK LIKE

I GAVE YOU ALL MY
THOUGHTS
NOW I LOST MY MIND

I AM STILL WORTHY

BE INTIMATE WITH MY
MIND
BEFORE MY BODY

THERE IS   GOOD   IN YOU

EVEN IF YOU HURT ME

THERE IS STILL GOOD IN ME

EVEN IF I HURT YOU

I WROTE YOU A LETTER,

I MIGHT
NEVER SEND IT.

WE HAVE SOMETHING
TO SAY WE WANT
TO SAY SOMETHING
TO EACH OTHER
~~WE SAY SOMETHING~~
BUT WE DON'T
SO WE NEVER KNOW
WHAT WE HAVE TO SAY

TOO MUCH

THE THOUGHT OF YOU
IS BITTERSWEET

DO I MISS YOU
           OR

DO I MISS
BEING WANTED BY
YOU

VULNERABILITY

is

COURAGEOUS

I CAN'T SEE YOU
BUT I KNOW YOU'RE WITH ME

BECAUSE, HONESTLY

I NEED

YOU

JESUS

(I AM WITH YOU)

(I'M STILL HERE)

(WITH

YOU)

I HOPE YOU'RE PROUD

OF ME

I can't save you or
make you stronger, but
I'll keep creating ~~a hope that~~ until
you find salvation and
courage somewhere
in the midst of it all.

All contents in this book were illustrated and written
by Melody Hansen. And digitally formatted by Michelle Fok.

Second Edition / February 2020